CHANGE
the WORLD

MORE "CHANGE THE WORLD" RESOURCES BY MIKE SLAUGHTER

Change the World:
Recovering the Message and Mission of Jesus
ISBN 978-1-4267-0297-6

Selections from Change the World
(24-page sampler, bundled in packages of 10)
ISBN 978-1-4267-1176-3

Change the World: A Study for Leadership Teams
DVD with Leader Guide: ISBN 978-1-4267-1012-4

Change the World: A Study for Small Groups
Participants' Book: ISBN 978-1-4267-1209-8
DVD with Leader Guide: ISBN 978-1-4267-1140-4

MIKE SLAUGHTER

CHANGE the WORLD

Daily Inspiration to Make a Difference

Abingdon Press / Nashville

CHANGE THE WORLD
DAILY INSPIRATION TO MAKE A DIFFERENCE

Copyright © 2011 by Abingdon Press
All rights reserved.

This book is printed on acid-free paper.

Library of Congress Cataloging-in-Publication Data

Slaughter, Michael.
   Change the world : daily inspiration to make a difference / Mike
Slaughter.
      p.   cm.
   ISBN 978-1-4267-1482-5 (pbk. : alk. paper)
   1. Meditations.   2. Christian life—Methodist authors.   3. Christianity
and justice—Meditations.   I. Title.
   BV4832.3.S535 2011
   248.4'87—dc22   2010051393

11 12 13 14 15 16 17 18 19 20—10 9 8 7 6 5 4 3 2 1

MANUFACTURED IN THE UNITED STATES OF AMERICA

CONTENTS

INTRODUCTION

Many Christians today profess faith in God, but they embody the values of the dominant culture. They possess a soft-secular worldview rather than the worldview of Jesus. These folks believe in God and profess Jesus, but they trust the materialistic values of secular culture. There is a better Way, and it is Jesus' Way!

The true message and mission of Jesus is this: to bring good news to the poor, release to the captives, and freedom to the oppressed. The gospel is good news for the poor. If it is not benefitting the poor and oppressed, then it is not the gospel. Jesus calls us, his followers, to serve "the least of these." He calls us to a lifestyle of sacrificial mission, giving ourselves with him for God's redemptive work in the world.

That is what this book is about: accepting the call to the radical lifestyle of discipleship—a lifestyle that has the power to change the world. As you make your way through six weeks' worth of daily readings, you will be encouraged to

> hear Christ's call
> love God's people
> become a disciple
> live simply
> spread the word
> serve courageously

Whether you read one devotion each day or spread them out over a longer period of time, you will come to see that the world's ability to discover the relevancy of the gospel depends on our willingness to fully embrace and live the biblical mandate to love like Jesus. Each reading ends with one or more reflective questions to help you reevaluate your priorities and habits and make new commitments to do the things that matter most to God.

I invite you to rediscover and reclaim the message and mission of Jesus and, in the process, to change the world.

HEARING CHRIST'S CALL

ON EARTH AS IT IS IN HEAVEN

"Your kingdom come, your will be done
on earth as it is in heaven."
(Matthew 6:10)

When we pray these words, do we really mean it? What we are asking is for God's rule and reign to become a reality here on earth, just as it is in heaven. This challenges many of the traditions and paradigms within Christianity today.

Jesus' hermeneutic—his way of interpreting the Scriptures—was considered heretical by the religious scholars of his day. Our faith practice has also become a distortion of Jesus' gospel of the kingdom of God. We often embrace a disembodied "saved for heaven" theology. We have overemphasized getting people into heaven to the neglect of getting heaven into earth. The greatness of Christianity should be measured not by how many profess to be Christians but by how many people are serving those Christ served.

3

Jesus only had 120 followers when he left planet earth. By most standards, his ministry would be deemed an utter failure. But Jesus used a very different measure. Jesus saw faith as an active verb and not a noun. His followers practiced what I call mission evangelism. They understood that the mission was not to get the world into the church but to get the church into the world!

As followers of Jesus Christ, we are to be actively engaged in meeting the needs and closing the gaps of disparities for the least of these. The world will see the relevance of the gospel when we fully embrace and live the biblical mandate to love like Jesus. John Wesley called it the demonstration of "social holiness."

Too often we Christians suffer from a numbers neurosis. Let's quit worrying about how many of us there are and focus on being the hands and feet of Jesus in our homes, communities, and the outermost places of the world. It is time for us to rediscover and reclaim the message and mission of Jesus!

What can you do today to make your faith a verb, rather than a noun? What will you do to put feet to your faith?

JESUS' MISSION

The Spirit of the Sovereign LORD is on me, . . .
to preach good news to the poor.
He has sent me to bind up the brokenhearted,
to proclaim freedom for the captives
and release from darkness for the prisoners,
to proclaim the year of the LORD's favor. (Isaiah 61:1-2)

You might say that these words from the prophet Isaiah were Jesus' mission statement. Jesus read these words in his inaugural message in his hometown. Isaiah had foretold "the year of the LORD's favor"—the dawn of the messianic kingdom—and Jesus proclaimed its arrival. Jesus' message focused on the kingdom of God's present influence in the world—a righting or restoration of God's created order on earth. He spoke not about going to heaven when we die, but about recognizing that heaven has come to earth.

When John sent word to Jesus from his prison cell, asking if he was truly the one who had been promised through the centuries by the prophets (Luke 7:18-19), Jesus did not go into a theological discourse. He simply pointed to the physical evidence of the presence of the power of God to complete the works of God: "Go back and report to John what you have seen and heard: The blind receive sight, the lame walk, those who have leprosy are cured, the deaf hear, the dead are raised, and the good news is preached to the poor" (Luke 7:22).

Jesus claimed to be the long-awaited Messiah whose presence would signify the arrival of God's kingdom and the restoration of all things. The evidence of his claims was not in his words but in the fruit of God's works. After Jesus read the passage from Isaiah 61, announcing the messianic presence in the synagogue in Nazareth, he dropped the big bombshell: "Today this scripture is fulfilled in your hearing" (Luke 4:21). The evidence was the direct intervention of God's heart and healing purpose in the lives of the poor and broken.

As followers of Jesus and citizens of the messianic kingdom, we are to continue Jesus' work. We are not to escape from the world's diseased brokenness but to engage the world and all those in it at the greatest places of need. We are not waiting for heaven but are actively rebuilding, restoring, and renewing the lives of broken people and shattered communities. Yes, we are waiting for the return of the King. But it is not passive waiting! As we wait, we are to faithfully demonstrate the good news of the kingdom by embracing a countercultural lifestyle—a visibly sacrificial lifestyle—that causes non-Christians to pay serious attention.

*In what ways is your lifestyle "countercultural"?
Think of one change you can make to begin living more
sacrificially for the sake of the kingdom.*

GOD'S FAVORED CHILD

Has not God chosen those who are poor in the eyes of the world to be rich in faith and to inherit the kingdom he promised those who love him? But you have insulted the poor.
(James 2:5-6)

Every parent is guilty of showing favoritism at times to one child over the other. Often, the child who appears to get the most attention from a parent is not the one for whom everything is going smoothly, but the one who is struggling the most or most troubled at the time. One of my children is a lot like me. She is strong-willed and determined. Those years between eleventh grade and her sophomore year in college were challenging to say the least. My son is more like his mother. He was very obedient and never really rebelled. But just because Kristen had our intense focus didn't mean that we loved her more or less than her brother. For a time she simply required more focused attention.

God, our Heavenly Parent, does not show favoritism, as Romans 2:11 reminds us. Yet in the Bible God clearly gives priority to the poor. Jesus affirms this priority in the parable of the Great Banquet (Luke 14). God's guests at the party ultimately become the poor, crippled, lame, and blind.

Why does God give such priority to the poor?

The world tends to determine and assign human "worth" based on what a person has—education, money, position, or influence. God, on the other hand, has a different value system. In the kingdom of God, a person has worth because of who he or she is—a child created in God's image. God does not value you more than another because you were born in a First World economy with all the luxuries it affords. The truth is, for two thirds of the world's population, poverty is simply the consequence of latitude and longitude—not the result of a lack of initiative. God loves and values the poor, and God wants us to have the same heart of compassion for those in need.

We have become calloused, indifferent, and insulated from the needs of our brothers and sisters lying at our doorstep. It's time to wake up and take a good look around us. The gap between the rich and the poor is growing. The global economic crisis that began in 2008 has only accelerated the erosion of the middle class. We are facing challenging times. Yet what an opportunity we have to rebuild, restore, and renew in devastated places! This is not a time to fear or to insulate ourselves from pain and suffering around us; it is a time to repent and realign our priorities and resources with the message and mission of Jesus.

What is one thing you can do to "show favor" to the working poor or homeless in your area?

CRUISE SHIP RELIGION

"Whoever wishes to be great among you must . . . be your slave; just as the Son of Man came not to be served but to serve, and to give his life a ransom for many."
(Matthew 20:26-28 NRSV)

Have you ever been on a cruise? A cruise is a hedonistic experience of extravagance and excess. Okay, so maybe I've never been on one, but my parents have gone on thirteen cruises in the last ten years. I feel vicariously bloated every time my dad talks about the buffets.

People choose a cruise for the experience of vacation and retreat. You expect to be served. After all, no one leaves a mint on your pillow in the evening or makes your bed in the morning when you are home. You work so hard all the other weeks of the year. You deserve to be pampered! On a cruise your involvement is totally based on self-interest. You can select from a seemingly endless menu of activities. Explore the interior of a tropical island, whale watch among the glaciers, or swim with the dolphins. Lie on a beach or snorkel among the exotic fish along a living coral reef. If you prefer, you never need to leave the boat. Rock climbing, golf lessons, theaters, and swimming pools are just a few of the opportunities that invite your time. The only requirement is plenty of money to cover the expenses!

Some Christians practice a kind of "cruise ship" religion. They expect to be served rather than to serve. They feel they've put in their time and deserve to sit back and let others do the work. They're interested in enjoying their religion and getting what they want from it. They're willing to give of themselves only when it is convenient and personally advantageous. And they tend to spend the majority of their money on themselves rather than giving sacrificially for the benefit of others.

The opposite of cruise-ship religion is servant discipleship—or mission evangelism. Mission evangelism is more like being in a mission outpost in a challenging place of great human need. Unlike life on a self-contained cruise ship, mission evangelism is outward focused, actively helping to meet the needs of the poor and marginalized through the church as it partners with social agencies, public schools, government and nongovernment organizations, and other faith groups. Mission evangelism is also experimental and flexible. Like Lewis and Clark mapping an uncharted route to the West, those who practice mission evangelism take risks and plan as they go.

In the words of Catholic theologian Hans Kung, "[We must] play down our longing for certainty, accept what is risky, and live by improvisation and experiment."[1] If we will get off the boat, follow where Jesus leads, and love as Jesus loved, we're guaranteed the adventure of a lifetime.

In what ways are you staying "in the boat" spiritually? What risk is God calling you to take in order to love others as he loves them? Tell a friend about it and ask him or her to hold you accountable.

THE GREAT REQUIREMENT

He has showed [all you people] what is good,
And what does the LORD require of you?
To act justly and to love mercy
and to walk humbly with your God. (Micah 6:8)

This verse tells us what God requires of us: to act justly, love mercy, and walk humbly with our God. But what does this mean?

First, God calls us to *do* justice—not to just believe in justice or study justice. We have power from God for our actions toward people, especially the poor and marginalized.

Justice is a core biblical theme. The very foundation of God's kingdom is established on justice (Psalm 89:14). As followers of Jesus, we must always speak and act on behalf of those who lack voice or influence. We must go where Jesus is going, do what Jesus is doing, and be who Jesus is being for the orphan and widow.

This requires our involvement in the political process. We must be political for the sake of giving voice and vote to those who are denied, but we must repent of our partisanship. No political party speaks for Jesus and his kingdom. As his followers, we stand in a prophetic tension with the systems and ideologies of the world. How then are we to engage politically?

It is not enough to just donate money and send aid. The church has been guilty far too many times of passivity and even participation in the injustices that have robbed people of dignity and destroyed human lives. Followers of Jesus must never stand idly by in the face of injustice but must work tirelessly to do justice.

Second, we are to be living demonstrations of God's mercy. Mercy is closely related to grace—receiving what one doesn't deserve or hasn't earned. God accepts us, demonstrated through the redemptive offering of his son on the cross, in spite of our brokenness and failures. Mercy is the generous demonstration of indescribable grace! Our call is to practically demonstrate God's mercy to the people in our communities through acts of service that provide daily life necessities.

Third, we are to serve others humbly, regardless of cultural, political, moral, or creedal differences. We serve without expectation of return or self gain. This is what it means to walk humbly with God. It's not about us or for us. It's about serving Jesus in other people: "For I was hungry and you gave me something to eat" (Matthew 25:35).

THE GREAT COMMANDMENT

"This is my commandment, that you love one another as I have loved you. No one has greater love than this, to lay down one's life for one's friends." (John 15:12-13 NRSV)

As a follower of Jesus, you simply cannot live out this mandate and stay in comfortable places. Loving others as Jesus loved requires sacrifice.

Every day, followers of Jesus Christ venture out into uncomfortable places to act in love for people they've never before met. The tremendous work of rehabilitation in the aftermath of Hurricane Katrina is just one of many examples. Ginghamsburg Church has sent well over fifty work teams in the last five years since the devastating catastrophe hit New Orleans and the Gulf area. Some of our people have given up their vacation weeks to return as many as four and five times. People spend their Thanksgiving and Christmas breaks lifting the hopes and restoring the residences of those who have been ripped off by insurance companies and contractors. They do it because they are compelled by the love of Jesus.

Can you imagine how the world would be different if Christians everywhere—A.K.A. the church—stopped doing what Jesus commanded us to do? Think of all the economies and social services that would be affected due to the loss of unpaid servant labor and financial resources: schools, clinics, daycares, counseling centers, intervention and faith-based programs, homeless shelters, food pantries, GED programs, senior programs . . . Need I go on? The church is the largest nongovernment/nonprofit social agency in the United States.

How would your community be different if your church closed its doors tomorrow? What difference would it make if you and the other Christians you know stopped loving others after the example of Jesus?

Jesus calls us to make sacrifices—of our time, our money, our comfort—to serve others. "Whoever wants to save his life will lose it, but whoever loses his life for me and for the gospel will save it," Jesus says (Mark 8:35). Jesus never said it would be easy, but Jesus lost his own life for our sake to show us that self-sacrificial love really can change the world.

What hard thing is God calling you to do? What will you have to sacrifice in order to follow that calling?

THE GREAT COMMISSION

"All authority in heaven and on earth has been given to me.
Therefore go and make disciples of all nations, baptizing
them in the name of the Father and of the Son and of the
Holy Spirit, and teaching them to obey everything I have
commanded you." (Matthew 28:18-20)

Jesus has commissioned us to go and make disciples "of all." This requires us to serve without expectation, honoring all people as children who are created in God's image. We must work outside all walls, barriers, and limitations to promote God's justice through the demonstration of generous and practical acts of mercy. We must live Christlike lifestyles of sacrifice and simplicity that demonstrate the love of God revealed in the cross. Of course, this is all to no avail if we are not actively committed to building authentic Christ followers—disciples. And yet we cannot build authentic disciples unless we demonstrate the love of God revealed in the cross.

Making and building authentic disciples requires an authentic witness. In other words, we must present a "right" or true picture of Jesus and the Christian faith. Unfortunately, as David Kinnaman's research in *Unchristian: What a New Generation Really Thinks About Christianity* reveals, the most common reaction to Christianity by those outside the church is that Christians no longer represent what Jesus was really about. Christianity, they say, is not what it was meant to be. One respondent observed: "Christianity has become bloated with blind followers who would rather repeat slogans than actually feel true compassion and care."[2]

The majority of people who avoid Christianity don't see how Christians make a positive difference in the world. One person wrote, "I know what they are against but I don't know what they are for. It seems like the Christians I know are even against being proactive in environmental care." Many express the perspective that Christianity has been reduced to abstract ideas, rituals, rules, and "boring gatherings."

The book of James reminds us that the truest expression of worship we can offer God is to serve the poor and live the Jesus ethic: "Religion that God our Father accepts as pure and faultless is this: to look after orphans and widows in their distress and to keep oneself from being polluted by the world" (James 1:27). If we are to present an authentic witness of what Jesus Christ and Christianity are about, we must be actively involved in serving the most vulnerable.

Only by practically engaging our community at the places of greatest need will we demonstrate that the gospel is good news for the poor and that God is Father to the fatherless (Psalm 68:5).

We cannot "go and make" unless we are willing to go and serve.

> *If you were the only Christian your non-Christian friends knew, what would they think Jesus and Christianity are about?*

LOVING GOD'S PEOPLE

PROUD TO BE A CHRISTIAN?

*Since God loved us so much, we also ought to love one
another. . . . If we love one another, God lives in us, and
his love is perfected in us. . . . Those who say, "I love
God," and hate their brothers or sisters, are liars; for those
who do not love a brother or sister whom they have seen,
cannot love God whom they have not seen.*
(1 John 4:11-12, 20 NRSV)

A while back, I received this e-mail from a Jesus follower who was growing uncomfortable with the
"Christian" label.

> I used to call myself a Christian. Yet over the last 4-5
> years, I am leaning toward renouncing my Christianity.
> It all started with the 2004 election and the way the
> "evangelicals" turned that election into a battle of
> "family values." I work with so many people from so
> many different cultures, religions, and backgrounds, and
> many of them I have found to be beautiful people—

people that I love with all of my heart and soul and people that I call my family. One of them is a Muslim, yet so many fault me for accepting this person because of his religion. We share the human experience! A person may be gay, Jewish, Muslim, atheist, etc. I search to know that person by their heart. The more I experience "Christianity" these days the more I want to run far and fast from Christians.

Unfortunately, this e-mail is representative of many I have received. In their own words, people echoed the observation of Mohandas Gandhi: "I like your Christ, I do not like your Christians. Your Christians are so unlike your Christ."

Can we blame them? They have seen how many Christians gravitate to churches that embrace their personal political persuasions, excluding from true fellowship anyone who doesn't see eye to eye. They have witnessed elections in which people's allegiances have been drawn along partisan political ideologies rather than Christ-infused theology. They have listened as the "Christian" extreme radio pundits of the airwaves have proclaimed God's anointed and defamed the heretical. This spirit of disdain and exclusion prevents many from experiencing the resurrected Christ and drives others away.

As Jesus' followers, we are to be committed to relationships of integrity and truth. But somewhere along the way, we've lost sight of the Spirit of the One who embodies truth. Like the Pharisees, we may know the letter of the law while missing the Spirit of God's intent.

Given the exclusivity with which many Christians interpret Christ's message, perhaps we can begin to understand why there is such indifference and even hostility toward Christians and Christianity today. The question is, what will we do about it?

Are you aware of common objections and criticisms people have about Christianity and Christians? Talk to non-Christians. Find out what the negative perceptions are, why they exist, and what you can do to help reverse them.

READING THE BIBLE
AS JESUS DID

"I have much more to say to you, more than you can now bear. But when he, the Spirit of truth, comes, he will guide you into all truth." (John 16:12-13)

Jesus made a pointed critique of the religious leaders of his day that still applies today: "You have let go of the commands of God and are holding on to the traditions of men" (Mark 7:8). All of us bring to the interpretation of Scripture certain prejudices. We experience life through the window of our life experiences, culture of origin, and family value systems. Each of us brings a blend of political ideology, personal prejudice, and folk religion, mixing it in with some scriptural truth to form a personalized system of life doctrines. What we emphatically proclaim as God's absolute law is nothing more than our version of Israel's golden calf.

We simply cannot begin to grasp the eternal wisdom of the written word apart from an ongoing relationship with the living Word, Jesus. As we follow Jesus, we need to continually seek the wisdom and guidance of his living Spirit. Because God is fully revealed in Jesus, all Scripture must be interpreted through and in the Spirit of Jesus.

When reading Scripture, we must ask ourselves, *How is this like God who is revealed in Jesus?* Many parts of the Bible are descriptive but not meant to be prescriptive—that is, not meant for us to "go and do likewise." If we were to view many of the conquest passages of the Old Testament as commands by God to wipe out innocent people, then we would have a theology like that of the radical religious terrorists of the world.

Jesus said, "You have heard that it was said, 'Love your neighbor and hate your enemy.' But I tell you: Love your enemies and pray for those who persecute you, that you may be sons of your Father in heaven" (Matthew 5:43-45). The way of Jesus is a higher way. His followers willfully choose life over condemnation. When the woman caught in the act of adultery was brought to Jesus, the teachers of the law and Pharisees demanded that she be given the justice that "the Law of Moses" demands (John 8:2-11). But Jesus showed her mercy and compassion. He did not follow the letter of the law. He fulfilled the spirit of the law.

When reading the Bible, we must look beyond the letter of the word to the Spirit of the Word.

Read a passage of Scripture and ask yourself, "How is this like God who is revealed in Jesus?" Make this your habit whenever reading Scripture.

TOXIC RELIGION

Jesus said to him, "Get up! Pick up your mat
and walk." At once the man was cured;
he picked up his mat and walked.
The day on which this took place was a Sabbath, and so the
Jews said to the man who had been healed, "It is the Sabbath;
the law forbids you to carry your mat." (John 5:8-10)

During a Jewish festival, Jesus stopped by Bethesda, a spa that people with disabilities frequented for the perceived healing properties in the pools. He talked with a man who had been experiencing a form of paralysis for thirty-eight years. This man had laid claim to his place alongside the pool, but his physical state remained unchanged. Jesus asked him the question that precipitates all healing and life change: "Do you really want to get well?" He commanded the man to "Get up, pick up your mat, and walk." Amazingly, the man got up and did what had seemed impossible—he walked!

Here is where toxic religion enters the picture. The Jewish leaders told the man it was against the law to carry his mat on the Sabbath. They began persecuting Jesus and trying to kill him, not only because he was breaking the Sabbath but also because he was calling God his Father and making himself equal with God (John 5:16-18). Rather than celebrating the man's healing, they rejected the man and his healer for not adhering to the religious code they embraced. They valued rules over people and felt justified in their exclusion.

Have you ever been burned by toxic religion or religious people? *Toxic* means "deadly." Toxic religion affects our understanding of who God is. It causes us to perceive God as being critical, unapproachable, and inaccessible. Most people I know believe in God but struggle with the idea that God believes in them. Because of how Christians have treated them in the past, they're convinced that God has rejected them too. In the pain of failure we tend to run and hide from God, but God doesn't reject or run away from us!

Because of our toxic understanding of God, we seek life from non-life-giving sources—a clandestine relationship, addictive substances, unhealthy eating. People turn to these sources not because they don't believe in God, but because of the toxins that come from God's people. Jesus refers to these toxins as the yeast of the Pharisees. The gospel means good news. But for many people, their perception of the gospel is not good news but a gospel of "you can't do that!"

As human beings, we tend to focus on rigid rules and rituals of exclusion. But Jesus wants us to have a right understanding of God, who is Life, Love, Grace, and Truth.

Do you have any toxic ideas about who God is? Examine the life of Jesus in the Gospels and remember that he is the perfect representation of who God is. Look for an opportunity to share this good news with someone else today.

ONE BIG HAPPY FAMILY

"Pray then in this way:
Our Father in heaven, . . ."
(Matthew 6:9 NRSV)

These words contain possibly the most revolutionary understanding about God that Jesus introduced: God is our Father! God is not exclusive to one tribe or nation; God is Father of all nations, tribes, and peoples.

On the day of Pentecost (the birthday of the church) the Spirit of God was not given until God-fearing people were gathered "from every nation under heaven" (Acts 2). The list is truly amazing in its inclusivity. God was even inclusive in language. Everyone heard the word in his or her own native tongue. The first Christians were Jews. And guess what? Arabs were also invited to the party. Even the Cretans are mentioned, and they were on the top of everyone's list of folks you don't want to live next door! God truly wants us to be one big happy family.

Sometimes it's difficult for us to experience God as our loving Father who accepts us and has a plan and purpose for us. Think about it. What happens when you find yourself coming over a rise on the highway and you see a police officer on the side of the road? Even if you're traveling under the speed limit, you immediately hit the brakes. The response is subconscious and involuntary. There are many places I want to see police, but never when I'm traveling down the highway. It's the same in our encounters with God. We don't want to run into a cosmic cop when we're heading down life's highway. Guilt creates subconscious avoidance. But a loving, all-powerful parent is different. Unfortunately, we've all experienced in some way the toxins of religious teachings that portray God more as a condemning authority than a loving Father who disciplines us in our failures because he wants us to experience future health and success.

If you're a parent, you understand to some degree the love and acceptance God feels toward us. I can't think of any failure so great that it would cause me to banish my children from my life. They could choose to walk away from my love and provision, but I would not give up on or forsake them. God is the God of love and our perfect loving Parent. How, then, as God's children can we be unloving, mean-spirited, and exclusive?

After a person passes the age of fifty, periodic tests are needed for cancer screening. However, there is one cancer that goes easily undetected and requires regular self-exams:

the cancer of a judgmental spirit. The judgmental demons of divisiveness have no place among God's children. We are to be an inclusive, global family driven by God's redeeming love.

Do you have a judgmental spirit toward someone or some group of people? Imagine if that person or people were actually your biological siblings. Treat them with familial love and acceptance, because in God's eyes, they really are our brothers and sisters.

THE ROYAL LAW

If you really keep the royal law found in Scripture,
"Love your neighbor as yourself," you are doing right.
But if you show favoritism, you sin and are convicted
by the law as lawbreakers.
(James 2:8-9)

Exactly who is my neighbor? This question was asked of Jesus, and he told a simple story to answer it.

A man was beaten by robbers and left for dead on the road. Two religious folk went past without stopping. (Not much has changed, has it? Christians continue to "drive by" places of pain and suffering if for no other reason than we don't know what to do.)

Then Jesus' story took a pointed turn. "But a Samaritan . . . came where the man was; and . . . took pity on him" (Luke 10:33). For the religious Jew, the phrase "good Samaritan" would have been an oxymoron. Samaritans were a mixed race, being the descendants of the Babylonian captors and the Jewish remnant that had not been deported during the time of captivity. They were considered "unclean" because of their mixed heritage. Samaria was located between Judea in the South and Galilee in the north. So, a righteous Jew traveling from the north or south would actually go around Samaria to avoid contact with "unrighteousness." Yet it was this unrighteous Samaritan whom Jesus used as the illustration of righteousness.

Jesus asked:

> "Which of these three do you think was a neighbor to the man who fell into the hands of robbers?"
> The expert in the law replied, "The one who had mercy on him."
> Jesus told him, "Go and do likewise." (Luke 10:36-37)

Jesus was saying that right action trumps right doctrine. Yes, truth matters, but God's truth is always demonstrated through loving, redemptive actions.

James' reference to the "royal law found in Scripture" refers to the law belonging to the King. The religious Jew was committed to the keeping of over 600 commandments. Jesus summarized all these duties in one: "A new command I give you: Love one another. As I have loved you, so you must love one another" (John 13:34). God has created us as relational beings. We are made to live in trusting relationships of health and fidelity with God and one another. We love and serve God when we love and serve one another.

We are Christ's body in the world. We are the only hands

Jesus has to rebuild in broken places. We are his only feet to march in the war against poverty and injustice. We are his only voice to share the good news of eternal life and offer hope to the hopeless. Our bank accounts are the only fiscal resources he has to carry out the Father's mission.

If we don't take action, who will? It's time to keep the royal law.

How can you be an unexpected neighbor to someone in need this week—someone you don't know and might not otherwise help? Watch for an opportunity, and enlist others to accompany you, if necessary.

GOD OF SECOND CHANCES

Look after each other so that none of you fails to receive the grace of God. (Hebrews 12:15 NLT)

I was always among the youngest in my class, trailing behind in both maturity and coordination. I had the attention span of the family dog. My fourth-grade teacher failed me, but the principal overrode that decision, passing me to fifth grade. This was my first memorable experience of grace—receiving what I had not deserved or earned.

My life would look much different today if it hadn't been for that gift of grace. I would not have met my wife when she came home from college to student teach while I was working with the church youth group. My children and grandchild would not be here, and they would not have affected countless other peoples' lives. I would not have been sent to Ginghamsburg Church in 1979 because I would have been one year behind, and that little congregation might have died out rather than becoming a catalyst for mission to God's people worldwide. How different the world would be if that principal had not made that small, gracious decision.

Like my principal, God is the God of second chances. Just look at God's list of "who's who" in the Bible. Most of them were screw-ups! Moses had an anger management problem that resulted in manslaughter. David had a sexual obsession that led to a Mafioso-style hit on one of his officers. The Bible is not a book about righteous people who serve as heroic examples; it's about a gracious God who uses us in spite of our brokenness and never lets go until we become who God created us to be.

A genealogy in the Gospel of Matthew reveals the scope of God's outrageous grace. Perez, the son of Judah and Judah's daughter-in-law Tamar, was conceived in the arms of deception and distorted passion that would make the scenarios of *Desperate Housewives* seem tame. (You can read the details in Genesis 38.) Talk about grace! These screwed up people are chosen to be in the DNA line of the Messiah.

I'm thankful our God is a God of second chances! We're called to share that same grace with others. Sometimes it's hard to live in the paradox of grace and truth, but Jesus warned us about the dangers of self-righteousness. Self-righteousness gives us spiritual blindness, making us oblivious to our own brokenness and magnifying the failures of others. We must remember that righteousness is not earned; it's the result of God's redemptive work in the cross. When we judge others, we demean the redemptive work of Jesus and make it our own.

Let's look after one another and freely share the grace of God. May we be people who always give second chances.

Can you recall a time when you were given a second chance? Make a difference in the life of someone in need of grace by offering acceptance, inclusion, and love despite the person's brokenness or failure.

HOLDING GRACE AND TRUTH IN BALANCE

The Word became flesh and made his dwelling among us.
We have seen his glory, the glory of the One and Only, who
came from the Father, full of grace and truth. (John 1:14)

When people's experience of God through other Christians is one of rigid laws and judgmental condemnation, they run the danger of going to the opposite extreme. Attempting to escape rigid legalism, some dive into the quagmire of relativism, which says, "You're not the boss of me; I'm the boss of me. I can do whatever I want." Those who err in this extreme end up seeking the god they want rather than the God who is. God is a moral God, and God has established absolute moral boundaries or laws—just as God has established absolute natural laws.

When I was growing up, I loved spending time at my grandparents' home. My friend Jimmy, who was a year older and more experienced in the mischievous adventures of the world, lived next door. One day we were commenting on the new Mary Poppins movie. Jimmy knew for a fact that if we took my grandfather's black umbrella with the cane handle, we could jump off the roof of his garage and float safely to the ground. I'm glad Jimmy jumped first! The umbrella immediately inverted, and Jimmy broke his wrist on the hard concrete driveway. That day I learned that gravity is an absolute law that applies to all, whether or not you believe it.

God designed the universe setting forth certain physical and moral truths. These are absolute; God is a God of truth. But God is also a God of grace. While we seek to demonstrate God's truth in the world, we must remember that we are fallible and not qualified to judge others based on our understanding of God's truth. We must practice grace as we seek to walk in God's truth. This balance was demonstrated most perfectly in and through Jesus—God incarnate. Jesus was the Word that became flesh and came from the Father, "full of grace and truth."

Toxic religion disrupts the balance of grace and truth. It goes to extremes, focusing either on truth apart from grace, or on grace without acknowledgement of absolute truth. Healthy religion holds the two in balanced tension. This balancing act requires the ability to recognize the difference between being judgmental and being spiritually discerning. Judgment produces anger, criticism, and slander. Judgment is exclusive and gives us a smug sense of satisfaction over another's failure. Discernment, on the other hand, creates empathetic pain that leads to compassion and intercession. The Spirit of discernment connects us to the heart and patience of God.

A growing number of Christians are seeking to avoid the extremes of legalism and relativism. They are seeking to hold grace and truth in balanced tension. And in so doing, they are reclaiming the radical and inclusive message of Jesus Christ.

> *Do you tend to exercise judgment or discernment? Check the fruit in your life. Judgment produces anger, criticism, slander, arrogance, and exclusion. Discernment produces compassion, intercession, patience, acceptance, and inclusion. When you're tempted to judge, pray for the spiritual discernment to see the person or situation through God's eyes, and let the Spirit guide your response.*

BECOMING A DISCIPLE

A WAY OF LIFE

*All of the believers were together and had everything in
common. Selling their possessions and goods, they gave to
anyone as he had need. Every day they continued to meet
together in the temple courts. They broke bread in their
homes and ate together with glad and sincere hearts, praising
God and enjoying the favor of all the people. And the Lord
added to their number daily those who were being saved.*
(Acts 2:44-47)

Reread the last sentence of this passage from Acts. Did
you catch it? People were drawn to this group of believers—the first church. They did not see them as judgmental
or hypocritical. People saw the demonstration of a lifestyle
that was focused on others and committed to unselfish service. Those who made the commitment to follow the one
who could not be defeated by death were willing to follow
in his footsteps and pay, if necessary, the ultimate price of
sacrifice for the success of God's mission.

Discipleship is a way of life that imitates Jesus. Disciples of Jesus Christ live and reflect the values, priorities, and lifestyles of the kingdom. It is possible to attend church regularly without ever becoming a true disciple. In fact, often our focus on church attendance and "numbers" is the very thing that distracts us from discipleship. Being transformed into a disciple of Jesus Christ requires much more than church attendance; it requires regular spiritual disciplines such as Scripture reading, prayer, journaling, accountability, giving, service, and witness.

John Wesley had the people called Methodists practice daily "methods" or disciplines. He saw how people could quickly become converted through enthusiastic preaching and just as quickly fall away if they were not committed to daily practices and accountability groups or classes. More and more people were bringing Jesus into their worldview instead of being transformed into his.

Now, don't misunderstand me. I believe that attending church is important, and that we must reach new people. There is a lost world to be saved! However, Jesus calls us to be and to make *disciples*, not church attendees.

Discipleship is a commitment to a way of life. It is commitment to a life-changing and lifelong process of growth.

How has following Jesus impacted or changed your lifestyle—the way you live your life? Are you growing as a disciple, becoming more and more like Jesus? Recommit to the practice of regular spiritual disciplines. Which discipline(s) do you need to restart or renew? Choose one to focus on this month.

MOTORCYCLE MANTRA

Do not merely listen to the word, and so deceive yourselves.
Do what it says. (James 1:22)

I wanted a motorcycle from the time I was a teenager, but other priorities delayed such recreational nonessentials. Finally, after saving for almost ten years, I ordered my lava red 2005 Harley-Davidson Road King Custom.

I soon discovered that while there are 600 factors you need to take into account when driving an automobile, there are 2,400 factors you need to take into account on a motorcycle. Bikers use the acronym SEE (Search, Evaluate, Execute) as the checklist for taking these risk factors into account. These same three practices can ensure our faithful navigation and completion of Christ's mission as disciples.

Search. A biker is always looking at the road about twelve seconds ahead. Where are the cavernous potholes, gravel, or wet leaves that mean little when driving a car but can send a biker over the handlebars? How will you approach the curve? These are things the driver of an automobile may not consciously see, but they can mean serious injury or even death for the biker if he or she is not focused on the road ahead.

Similarly, as disciples we must always be seeking the wisdom of God's word, listening to the intuitive voice of the spirit, and seeking the wise counsel of spiritual mentors to determine how to navigate the road ahead. We must seek first God's perspective on everything from money to marriage, understanding the world and our responsibility to it. We must know where God wants us to be tomorrow to determine our course of action today. We must have vision, a clear picture of God's preferred future, and then act on it.

Evaluate. When biking, I want to have a proactive plan of action before I get to the point of challenge in the road ahead. Likewise, discipleship is a commitment to self-awareness. As disciples, we must continually take a moral and spiritual inventory to ensure we are staying true to God's call. Identifying fellow disciples who will offer honest evaluation is also important.

Execute. James reminds us that we're blessed in what we do, not by what we merely hear or intellectually believe. Most people have the "want to," but few have the "work to." Life is not measured in words. Life happens in action. Jesus' invitation to his disciples was not first to believe in him but to follow him. Faith doesn't precede the journey; it grows out of the journey. As disciples, we must make a commitment to the rigors of the daily journey with Jesus.

Search. Evaluate. Execute. It's a good mantra not only for bikers but also for disciples of Jesus Christ.

What spiritual "potholes" do you see in your own life?
Evaluate how you will handle these challenging situations
when they arise. How will you prepare yourself to execute
your plan when the moment comes?

VOLUNTEER OR SERVANT?

"Whoever serves me must follow me, and where I am, there will my servant be also. Whoever serves me, the Father will honor." (John 12:26 NRSV)

Are you a volunteer or a servant? If you're not sure, consider these definitions: Volunteers serve at their own convenience, while servants serve at the discretion of the one who calls. This is a critical distinction for us to grasp.

In the early church, there were no "volunteers." There were only servant disciples. Doing ministry wasn't something Christians gave a few hours to each week. Rather, they devoted their lives to carrying on the mission and ministry of Jesus as directed and empowered by the Holy Spirit.

Today the idea of a servant disciple is foreign to many Christians; the more familiar concept is that of a volunteer. In many churches, the active work of missions, which once was done by servant disciples, is now assigned to paid church staff. Volunteers are often given the passive work of serving on committees or filling roles within the walls of the church. This shift is tragic, because we are transformed into disciples only as we are actively involved in the work of missions—as we respond to the call of Jesus to meet the needs of those in our communities and beyond.

Consider the first disciples; they learned and grew as they traveled and ministered with Jesus. They did not maintain the status quo, fitting ministry into their lives around other commitments; they committed their lives to ministry. They were willing to give up everything to follow Jesus, going wherever he led them and doing whatever he called them to do.

I like to say that everyone doing the work of the church is a servant. Some are "paid servants" and some are "unpaid servants," but we all serve with a fully devoted heart for meeting needs in Jesus' name. We do not become disciples by volunteering as it fits into our schedule. We become disciples by being dedicated servants who are committed to carrying on the work and mission of Jesus—regardless of the sacrifice required.

How can you get involved in hands-on missions work in your community or area? Identify what you can do to actively participate in existing ministries or outreach opportunities, or take steps to organize a new program or ministry that God may be calling you to start.

PRIESTHOOD OF ALL

Like living stones, let yourselves be built into a spiritual
house, to be a holy priesthood, to offer spiritual sacrifices
acceptable to God through Jesus Christ. . . . You are a cho-
sen race, a royal priesthood, a holy nation, God's own peo-
ple, in order that you may proclaim the mighty acts of him
who called you out of darkness into his marvelous light.
(1 Peter 2:5, 9 NRSV)

Did you know that every follower of Jesus Christ is a priest? We're all ministers, whether or not we have been to seminary or have been ordained as clergy.

Even Jesus did not possess the pedigree for the official priesthood. He was from the tribe of Judah, and only those from the tribe of Levi could be priests. As a matter of fact, the Christian movement began without a professionally credentialed priesthood at all. Every follower was anointed and appointed by the Spirit to use the gifts that he or she was given for the benefit of Christ's body and mission.

As the church became more formalized and institutionalized, a two-tier caste system was created that separated "priest" and "parishioner." Slowly but surely the work of ministry became the responsibility of the priests—and eventually, of paid church staff. But this was not the original plan! Scripture says that we are a holy, royal priesthood set apart to communicate and carry out the mission of Jesus.

When Ginghamsburg Church had fewer than one hundred people, I was the only salaried staff person. Every hand was needed to accomplish the aggressive mission agenda that we were called to do. Peggy began the gently used clothing store; Sue started the food pantry. A local school teacher created one of the most mission-driven student ministry programs in the country. Two years later Mike became our second full-time staff person. Mary oversaw the newly formed cell group ministry; Lou created a children's program and later a preschool daycare. Dean directed our visitation and hospital teams, and Tom organized our mission teams. Randy put together four worship teams, and Rose led the prayer chain. Diane and Len nurtured seekers through the membership assimilation process. A church of less than 100 people had fifty to sixty disciples functioning as "ministers" with a budget of only $27,000 a year. That could not have been possible if the people had not stepped into their true identity as ministers of Jesus Christ.

As disciples, we should not need to be coerced to use our gifts for the benefit of Christ's body in ministering to the world. Rather, like the prophets and saints who have gone before us, we hear the voice of God asking, "Whom shall I send? And who will go for us?" And we willfully respond, "Here am I. Send me!" (Isaiah 6:8).

Have you ever felt unqualified to serve God? How is God calling you to use your gifts now, at this time in your life? How will you respond?

L.I.F.E. PURPOSE

"I came that they may have life, and have it abundantly."
(John 10:10 NRSV)

A friend gave me a GPS navigational device for my car. A human-sounding computerized voice directs you throughout the duration of your trip. You can choose the language and accent. The voice tells you when you have made a wrong turn and recalculates directions to get you back on course. As "smart" as this device is, there's one essential factor necessary for it to work: You must enter the destination before you begin the journey.

It's the same with our life mission. You must know the destination to fulfill your life destiny. God has created each of us with a purpose. David wrote in Psalm 139: "For you created my inmost being; / you knit me together in my mother's womb. / . . . All the days ordained for me / were written in your book / before one of them came to be" (vv. 13, 16). Life purpose is discovering why you're alive and knowing the contribution that you want to leave behind.

Some people confuse life purpose with goals, such as getting an education, succeeding in a career, being married, or raising a family. But goals are worthless unless you have a defining life mission that brings all your goals together.

The acronym L.I.F.E. can be used as a simple tool to discover your life purpose.

L-ove. *What do you love? What are you passionate about?* Soren Kirkegaard said that understanding what God wants you to do is about finding the idea for which you can live or die. It is through the deep passions in the recesses of your life that God speaks.

I-nfluences. *Who are the key influencers and influences in your life that have helped shape your understanding of who and whose you are?* After taking a course in college that dealt with issues such as poverty, race relations, and the environment, I transferred to the school of social work. The passion of that class has been a significant influence in shaping my life mission.

F-aith. *In what do you place your faith? What is the core reality or truth at the core of your center?* This truth is the determining factor in all your life priorities and decisions. Dependence on God's presence and promise of provision are the keys for a successful life mission.

E-xperience. *What are you really good at?* You don't need to change geographic locations, churches, spouses, or skill sets. God uses all of your life experiences, influences, passions, and skills to fulfill his mission in your life. God wants to do something in the world that is unique through you.

Remember, Jesus came that we may have LIFE abundant!

What is your life purpose? Write the acronym L.I.F.E. vertically on the left side of a sheet of paper, and write about what you love, who or what has influenced you, what truths lie at the center of your faith, and what lessons your experience has shown you.

RADICAL PRIORITIES

"Blessed rather are those who hear the word of God and
obey it." (Luke 11:28)

Commitment to Christ is not measured in belief but in action. Most Christians believe in God, but they don't trust God. They fear taking the risk of faith to do the work of faith.

Jesus said we are blessed when we obey God's word. We are not what we say; we are what we do. As Alan Hirsch wrote in his book *The Forgotten Ways*, we cannot "think our way into a new way of acting, but rather, we need to act our way into a new way of thinking."[3] Life is determined by our actions.

Jesus' encounter with the rich young entrepreneur gives insight into the commitment Christ requires of those who would follow him. The young man came to Jesus and asked, "What must I do to inherit eternal life?" Jesus began by listing biblical commandments that are foundational for relationship trust: "You shall not commit adultery; You shall not murder; You shall not steal; You shall not bear false witness; Honor your father and mother" (Luke 18:18, 20 NRSV). All relationships must be based in trust and have healthy, well-defined boundaries.

The man enthusiastically declared his commitment to biblical morality, but he stopped short of commitment to discipleship. Jesus made it clear that the call to discipleship goes beyond moralistic principles to a commitment of lifestyle change. "There is still one thing lacking," Jesus said. "Sell all that you own and distribute the money to the poor, and you will have treasure in heaven; then come, follow me" (Luke 18:22 NRSV).

Following Jesus calls for a radical reordering of priorities. Notice the discipleship process that Jesus was leading the young entrepreneur through: (1) selling/releasing the world's materialistic value system, (2) prioritizing the needs of the world's poor and oppressed, and (3) following Jesus in the way of sacrificial mission.

Many of us have professed Jesus but brought him into our own soft, secular, political worldviews instead of being converted into Jesus' worldview of the kingdom of God. The process of discipleship is moving from believers to followers; from donation to sacrifice; from moralistic principles to lifestyles of self-denial; from the pursuit of success to true significance. To be true disciples, we must learn to drop everything we have into the hands of Jesus so that we may be directed by God's purpose.

Do you need to radically reorder your priorities? Is there anything you need to sell or let go of? How can you let go of the world's materialistic values and make the needs of the world's poor and oppressed a greater priority?

FOLLOWING THE LEADER

Be imitators of me, as I am of Christ.
(1 Corinthians 11:1 NRSV)

Imprinting is a psychological term used to describe a specific life stage of learning. Primarily, it refers to animals that "imprint" on their parents and then learn important skills by following them around. The behavior of the parent is imprinted or downloaded in the prodigy. Konrad Lorenz showed how incubator-hatched geese would imprint on the first suitable moving stimulus they saw between the periods of thirteen to sixteen hours after hatching.[4] He used the example of young goslings imprinting to his boots and following his boots wherever he went. Young children seem to go through a similar process, even beginning to recognize the voices of their parents in the womb.

Likewise, we become disciples through the process of imprinting and following around. This is why it is so important for new or young Christians to have mature disciples they can look to as examples and guides. Health replicates health, and disease spreads disease. For better or worse, we infect people through our spiritual DNA. There are four qualities that a mature disciple should demonstrate in order to lead others. People who possess these qualities are discipleship leaders.

Engaged. Discipleship leaders should be actively engaged in the life and mission of the local church. They should be observed in a frontline ministry over a period of time and have demonstrated effectiveness with measurable results.

Inspired. Discipleship leaders need to be inspired with the vision of the pastor and the mission of the local church, and they must inspire others. Leaders are leaders because they are contagious. They are people that others are readily listening to and following. If you think you are a leader, just look back over your shoulder. If no one is following, then guess what?

Informed. Discipleship leaders need to be informed about the twenty-first century church and its mission. They understand the investment of time and resources involved for training and are willing to make commitments to the process of lifelong learning.

Invested. Discipleship leaders are vested in the kingdom mission, not just with their time and energy, but also with their financial resources. Followers will imprint the stewardship habits of their leaders. There have been many talented, gifted people that I have overlooked for positions of influence over the years because they failed in this critical area. The disciple honors Jesus with the first fruits of the tithe and then sacrificially follows with sacrificial offerings motivated through love.

Every disciple needs a credible source of authority— someone to look to for leadership and guidance. Those who make effective discipleship leaders are engaged, inspired, informed, and invested. They humbly invite others to follow them as they follow Christ.

Who are your spiritual mentors—those individuals who provide spiritual leadership, guidance, and encouragement? Do they possess the four qualities of a discipleship leader? Who is following you? Are you demonstrating the four qualities for them to imitate?

LIVING SIMPLY

A SIMPLER TIME

A pretentious, showy life is an empty life;
a plain and simple life is a full life.
(Proverbs 13:7 The Message)

In the early years of our marriage, Carolyn and I lived in a three-room cinder block duplex with no insulation or drywall. When it was hot outside, it was an oven inside. In January there was frost on the walls inside. We had very little money, but Carolyn was masterful at making a $20-a-week grocery budget work in the 1970s. It's amazing how many variations there are on tuna casserole! The floor was 1946 linoleum. We found remnants of orange shag carpeting to cover the floors, and painted crates that served as end tables and bookcases. My grandparents gave us a table that had been in their cellar, and we bought directors' chairs for living room furniture. Despite our shabby abode, Carolyn and I look back at those times as a reminder that full and abundant life consists not of the things we possess but of the relationships in which we invest.

The recent global recession is likewise teaching Americans that bigger isn't necessarily better and less can be more. Americans' pursuit of megalifestyles in the last several decades created an unsustainable debt cycle. Americans reached a negative savings rate in 2005, spending $1.22 for every $1.00 earned. We craved houses we could not afford and the latest digital gadgets we didn't need. Bankers were willing to fuel unbridled appetites with subprime interest loans. Our 401(k)s were soaring due to an overvalued stock market. The Dow Jones Industrial Average, which crossed 14,000 in 2007, fell to nearly 6,500 in 2009. Struggling American car manufacturers became paralytic when gas prices soared to more than $4.00 a gallon in the summer of 2008. They had failed to heed the economic warning signs and continued to build the mammoth gas guzzlers that the American appetite craved.

Now more people are using public transportation. We are driving less and keeping our cars longer. Mortgage-strapped families are finding ways to downsize homes. Layoffs and salary freezes are forcing the majority of us to downsize our lifestyles, and we are beginning to spend less than we earn once again.

The economic malaise has caused us to look for ways to simplify our lives. Many of us are rediscovering state parks as affordable and fun alternatives to expensive theme parks and resorts. "Simplicity" and "getting back to basics" are values we are reemphasizing. More and more of us are seeking ways to simplify and reduce clutter, and also to influence the world around us. We are embracing a simpler time—a time rich beyond measure.

> *What have you done to simplify your life, and*
> *what have been the results of these changes?*
> *What other steps can you take?*

MONEY MATTERS

*"Store up for yourselves treasures in heaven,
where neither moth nor rust consumes and where
thieves do not break in and steal. For where your
treasure is, there your heart will be also."*
(Matthew 6:20-21 NRSV)

Where we invest our money reveals the true state of our hearts. Challenging economic times cause us to re-examine our hearts and our financial priorities and practices. If we're willing, hard times help us figure out what's really important and how to manage our money according to God's priorities.

As followers of Jesus Christ, anything less than God's will in every dimension of our financial lives is not an option. We must say, "Lord, I want what you want, and by the strength that comes through your grace, I'm willing to work at it until I do it." This is the first step in getting our financial lives in order and moving toward a simpler, more generous lifestyle.

Once we have right priorities, we're ready to add right actions. I'd like to suggest seven actions that can help to get our financial houses in order, enabling us to live more simply so that others may simply live.

1. *Practice planned giving toward God's kingdom work.* It's impossible to seek after things and God at the same time (see Matthew 6:24). When we trust God's love and provision, we recognize God's ownership and willingly release our resources to Jesus' lordship.

2. *Seek wise counsel through an accountability group or counselor.* Because so many temptations come against us in the area of finances, we need the accountability of a financial counselor or group (many churches and community programs offer financial instruction and accountability through classes and small groups).

3. *Write or rework a budget.* With a budget, you are making a commitment to know where your money goes and make adjustments in the areas where you are overspending. *Everyone* needs a budget.

4. *Perform plastic surgery and reduce your debt.* Cutting up your credit cards is a commitment to an aggressive debt reduction program. To be faithful and obedient with what God has given you, you must deal with your debt.

5. *Set future goals and practice delayed gratification.* When we buy what we cannot afford, we're not practicing faith in God's word. We're essentially saying, "I don't

want to wait for a future blessing; I want it now." One of the most powerful disciplines of faith is the discipline of delayed gratification.

6. *Nurture an attitude of gratitude*. The apostle Paul wrote, "I have learned to be content with whatever I have. I know what it is to have little, and I know what it is to have plenty" (Philippians 4:11-12 NRSV). Be grateful for what you have and practice contentment.

7. *Pray, pray, pray*. The most important right action you can take is prayer. Prayer acknowledges that we are dependent upon God and that we trust God to lead, guide, and provide.

Is your financial house in order? What actions do you need to take to rightly manage your money?

FAMILY BUDGET

Honor the LORD with your wealth.
(Proverbs 3:9)

Everyone needs a budget! A budget helps you to know where your money goes and thereby to spend less than what you make. Only when you spend less than what you make are you able to give generously to others.

One of the simplest ways to start a budget is to use the 10-10-80 formula. The first 10 percent of what you make goes to God. The next 10 percent goes into investing for your future—a savings account or other low-risk investment. You pay yourself after you pay God. The remaining 80 percent is what you have left for living expenses. These expenses might include categories such as mortgage/rent, utilities, groceries, transportation/gas, insurance, entertainment, spending money, gifts, medical expenses, and so forth.

Of course, you will need to rework how you distribute the 80 percent when there are income changes or adjustments, such as when there are cost of living increases due to inflation or fluctuations in the economy. Oftentimes reworking a budget will require you to make decreases in spending.

A helpful budgeting tool is the envelope method. You designate an envelope for every category in your budget, being sure to allow a savings category for future needs as well. Then you put money or a check for the budgeted amount in each envelope. Once that money is gone, it's gone! Using plastic isn't an option. You can use only the money in the envelopes, and you can't borrow from one envelope to pad another. If you are a little more disciplined, a computer program can be used in a similar way. But you have to keep up with your spending in each category and hold yourself accountable!

Carolyn and I have been doing this for years. If Christmas is coming up and we have $300 in the Christmas envelope (or in the Christmas category in the computer program), we know that's all we can spend. We are not people who will spend $1,000 to $2,500 at Christmas because we simply won't put it on plastic. That's our rule.

If we want to go on vacation, we try to put aside a hundred dollars or more a month, depending on the state of the economy. When I was paying $70 per tank to fill up my SUV, vacation savings had to decrease some. So, let's say that we are setting aside what we can for vacation, and when the time comes we have only $400 in the account or envelope designated for vacation. We're obviously not going to Florida! So we might do two nights in Gatlinburg instead.

Remember that God calls us to grow in our giving, which requires careful budgeting and living by the Spirit. As we are willing to simplify and live below our means, we will be able to give generously, bless the lives of others, and change the world.

Are you willing to create a budget that will allow you to live beneath your means and give more generously to others?

GIVING SACRIFICIALLY

Jesus, looking at him, loved him and said, "You lack one thing; go, sell what you own, and give the money to the poor, and you will have treasure in heaven; then come, follow me. . . . For the Son of Man came not to be served but to serve, and to give his life a ransom for many."
(Mark 10:21, 45 NRSV)

Simplifying our lives and living below our means enables us to give sacrificially for the welfare of others. Sacrificial giving extends beyond financial sacrifice to actual hands-on service with the least and the lost. We have to move out of our comfortable, secure environments into a hurting world to serve others. This involves three practices or habits.

First, we must focus on the needs of others and respond with acts of compassion—whether the need be around the corner or around the world. Getting involved in short-term mission trips, one-time or ongoing service projects, and various outreach ministries can have a life-changing impact, forever altering our worldview and lifestyle.

Second, we must serve people in the love and compassion of Jesus—without strings attached. In other words, we must serve and expect nothing in return, trusting the Spirit to open doors for opportunities to share the reason why we serve.

On a mission trip to Darfur, I was sitting under a tree with a group of Muslim sheiks and village elders in the shadows of a new school facility we had just built in the middle of a rebel stronghold. We had also just completed a vocational school for young men to train in woodworking, brick making, and electrician jobs. Young women are being taught sewing, weaving, and the art of microbusiness. Our nearby water yard will supply the needs of 22,000 people and their livestock. In the respite of the shade on a 122-degree June day, one of the men in the group stood and asked, "Why are you here? Why are you Christians helping us? Where are our Arab brothers? Where is Saudi Arabia? Dubai?" When we demonstrate the love of Jesus without an ulterior motive, we earn the right to share the reason why.

Third, we must be a positive "living witness" to non-Christians. Jesus said the world would know we are his disciples through the demonstration of his sacrificial love. People have grown weary of the hypocritical words, angry judgments, and nonresponsive actions of Christians in the face of human need, injustice, and alarming environmental changes. It is time to carry out the mission of Jesus—in our nation and in all the world—in a more positive light.

*How is Jesus calling you to give for the sake of others?
Here's a practical challenge: Whatever you spend on family
members for their birthdays or Christmas, give an equal
amount to missions work.*

COMMUNITY

And let us consider how to provoke one another to love and good deeds, not neglecting to meet together, as is the habit of some, but encouraging one another, and all the more as you see the Day approaching. (Hebrews 10:24-25 NRSV)

Simplicity relates not only to our lifestyles and our finances, but also to our relationships. People today are seeking the intimate, relational experiences that are found in a community as opposed to a crowd. They are looking for meaningful connections with others that also allow for local, environmental, and global contributions of significance, especially as they relate to social justice, poverty, and making a real difference in their local community and world.

Community of this kind is biblical. The first Christians met together in homes around meals—the breaking of bread together (Acts 2:42). A new depth of relationships among believers was possible outside the temple courts. The

Gospels are filled with stories of Jesus himself accomplishing his mission as he ate, taught, and healed within homes, not inside the temple's walls.

Community is also missional. In community, individuals hold one another to higher accountability for being Christ's means of grace and healing in the lives of others, including the mission of inviting nonchurched people to be part of the community.

Finally, community is essential to discipleship. It provides an environment in which real transformation can take place through accountability and encouragement. An intimate community has the ability to minister to persons going through difficult life experiences in a personal and personalized way that a larger group setting simply cannot.

Whether you prefer a group that meets together for spiritual exploration and growth or a group that is centered on a common interest or activity, you will find there is no substitute for the fellowship and support of other Christians who join together regularly in community.

> *Are you part of a relational community of Christians? If not, seek to become part of a small group of believers who meet together regularly. If you are part of such a group, how is this community making a difference in your life and the lives of others?*

INVESTING IN PEOPLE, NOT THINGS

"Do not worry about your life, what you will eat; or about your body, what you will wear. Life is more than food, and the body more than clothes. . . . Sell your possessions and give to the poor. . . . Be dressed ready for service and keep your lamps burning." (Luke 12:22-23, 33, 35)

Living simply allows us to shift our focus from things to people. It eliminates those things that keep us from being able to respond to needs as the Spirit leads. It enables us to be people on the move.

During the pilgrimage from Egypt to the Promised Land, God gave Moses specific instructions for a tabernacle-tent that would be representative of God's presence with the people in their wilderness journey. "Whenever the cloud lifted from over the tent, then the Israelites would set out; and in the place where the cloud settled down, there the Israelites would camp" (Numbers 9:17 NRSV).

The mobility and flexibility of the tabernacle-tent are God's metaphor for us as the body of Christ. Jesus' call to "follow me" is an invitation to journey. He calls us to go into all the world and make disciples. We must be willing to pick up and go—to take action. This means going where Jesus is going and doing what Jesus is doing in the world. We must let go of anything that threatens to tie us down and keep us from following Jesus in service to others.

Our church board has made three attempts to initiate a building program that would complete the master plan developed in 1993. Each time the Spirit has put in our spirits a yield sign saying, "That is not where I am going, but follow me to—"

In 2004 the "follow me to—" became Darfur. I had a vision of a child standing and pleading, "Come over to Darfur and help us." We established the Sudan Project (the sudanproject.org), committed to the development of sustainable agriculture, safe water, and children's protection and development programs. If we had invested massive funds in a building as planned, we would not have had the mobility to respond rapidly to what the United Nations has deemed the worst humanitarian crisis in the world. Listening to the voice of the Spirit allowed us to move with God in speed and to have significant impact in the lives of many.

Sometimes our belongings and the space we create to house them all can hold us back from giving generously and selflessly. Treasures can quickly become trappings if they keep you from following the Spirit wherever it may lead you.

We are a pilgrim people who are called to go where Jesus is going and do what Jesus is doing in the world. This is possible only if we make it our commitment always to invest in people rather than in things.

What stands in the way of you following the call of Jesus in your life? What adjustments do you need to make in order to invest in people, not things?

CLUTTER IN OUR HOMES
AND LIVES

"The ground of a certain rich man produced a good crop.
He thought to himself, 'What shall I do?
I have no place to store my crops.' "
(Luke 12:16)

Living environments that are cluttered and crammed with stuff are not practical, nor do they honor God. How can we justify spending excessively on homes that are far larger than we need and lots of stuff to fill those homes when one child dies every four seconds of a hunger-related cause? Will we continue to seek after more and more stuff while Jesus is calling us to follow him in costly, sacrificial discipleship? Let's reclaim and recommit to the mission of Jesus by eliminating the clutter in our homes and lives.

I challenge us to adopt what my friend Kim Miller has called a "mud 'n' spit theology." In John 9, Jesus combined a handful of mud and a mouthful of spit as a creative medium for miraculously giving sight to a blind man. Jesus used what he already had to provide what was so desperately needed. With this inspiration, we can press hard into the belief that more money, more space, and more things aren't what we need to make our surroundings and our lives meaningful and satisfying. All we need are just a few resources and a little creativity!

Ask yourself:

- What things can I do without? What is nonessential? What can be eliminated?
- What meaningless things and activities are wasting my time, energy, and resources?
- What do I need (as opposed to want), and where can I acquire these items for much less than retail price?
- What things or services am I purchasing that I can create or do myself?
- What can I repurpose or reuse?

Sure, repurposing and resourcefulness is not only economically and environmentally sound theology; it is a practical necessity in destabilizing economic times.

Look around you. How many people are living beyond their means, cluttering their lives with more stuff than they can use? Will change begin with you? All it takes is one healthy person who makes a commitment to simplify. Then, one by one, others will take note of the contentment and peace in your life and will choose to follow your lead.

Consider the questions above. What changes can you make to reduce clutter in your home, your heart, and your life?

SPREADING THE WORD

SHARING YOUR FAITH

"A new command I give you: Love one another. As I have loved you, so you must love one another. By this all men will know that you are my disciples, if you love one another." (John 13:34-35)

I was driving on the interstate one day when I saw a billboard that said "Jesus Is Real." I made the comment to the others who were riding in the car with me that even though the statement was true, it was trite. We Christians have mastered the art of benign slogans without demonstrating the sacrificial lifestyle of the true meaning of the words. The world will not understand the truth of Jesus by our billboard and bumper sticker slogans. That is not evangelism. There is a better way to share our faith.

Jesus said that people will know we are disciples if we love the way he loved. The Gospels show us time and again how Jesus demonstrated his love in practical ways, healing those who were sick, feeding those who were hungry, and being present with those in need of comfort. He taught us how to put others before ourselves, and commanded us to love even our enemies.

Others will see the reality of Jesus in the tireless, sacrificial, practical ways that we serve our neighbors—whether close at home or far away. When we spend our Saturdays repairing old cars so poor families have a way to get to work and the supermarket, when we use a week's vacation time to go to the coast and rebuild hurricane-damaged homes, when we use our talents to provide dental care or financial advice to people in need, we are demonstrating the practical reality of Jesus' redemptive love.

Our actions really do speak louder than our words. We can talk all day long about the love of Jesus and his sacrifice for us, but if people do not see that love and sacrificial generosity reflected in our actions, our words are empty and meaningless. We must embody Jesus' message with our whole lives.

When we serve others, we are like living billboards that testify to the truth of the gospel. What a powerful way to share our faith!

Do your actions match the gospel you share with your words? Through what practical demonstrations of love will you share your faith?

JUDGING OURSELVES

"Do not judge, or you too will be judged. For in the same way you judge others, you will be judged, and with the measure you use, it will be measured to you."
(Matthew 7:1)

Non-Christians often say that Christians are judgmental people. Jesus tells us that we are to be judging, but not judging of other people—judging of ourselves! God alone will determine the consequences of everyone's life decisions. You and I aren't qualified, because we all sin.

Do you remember the woman who was caught in the act of adultery? The Pharisees had evidence against her, and they brought the woman to Jesus and said, "Jesus, here is the book. The book says that this lady has earned stoning, execution by stoning. That's what this book says." The Pharisees had the right theology; adultery is wrong. But, they had the wrong spirit. Jesus asked them if any of them were sinless; only a truly sinless person has any right to judge the sins of others. The whole purpose of the Pharisees was condemnation, but the whole purpose of Jesus is redemption and restoration.

Consider also David. King David was called "a man after God's own heart." But anytime you begin to get confident in your own godliness, you begin to have a self-confidence and a self-strength, rather than a God dependence. David had an adulterous affair, the woman became pregnant, and then David had a "Tony Soprano" style of hit done on the woman's husband. Nathan the prophet wanted to confront David and say to David, "David, what you have done is evil in the eyes of God." But, you have to remember that David, as king, had the power to remove Nathan's head. So, Nathan came up with a story to illustrate David's sin. Nathan told a story of a rich guy and a poor guy. The rich guy had all kinds of herds of cattle and sheep, and the poor man had only a little lamb, which he raised in his house like a pet. The rich guy had visitors and took the poor guy's one single lamb and served it for dinner. Here is the problem with a judgmental spirit—David got incensed in anger and said, "That man must die!" And Nathan said, "David, that man is you!" (2 Samuel 12:7). When we are blind to our own brokenness, we are quick to condemn the sins of others.

People often ask, *What is God like?* When we look at Jesus, we see the face of God. God is like Jesus. God is not the vicious, condemning, angry god that so many picture. Instead he is merciful and forgiving and full of grace. But also, when we look at Jesus, we see who you and I are created to be. Let us examine ourselves, take stock of and address our own weaknesses. Toward other people, we should be gracious and nonjudgmental, a living testimony of God's grace to all people.

Does judgment of other people's sin or weakness blind you to your own sin? Make a daily practice of examining your own life for things you need to confront and address. How can you show grace to someone you have previously judged?

GETTING OUT OF YOUR COMFORT ZONE

[Jesus] said to Simon, "Put out into the deep water and let down your nets for a catch." Simon answered, "Master, we have worked all night long but have caught nothing. Yet if you say so, I will let down the nets." When they had done this, they caught so many fish that their nets were beginning to break. So they signaled their partners in the other boat to come and help them. And they came and filled both boats, so that they began to sink. (Luke 5:4-7 NRSV)

Jesus was teaching the crowds on the bank of the Sea of Galilee. Two boats were on the water's edge while the owners were cleaning their nets after a long night of fruitless labor. Jesus enlisted the fishermen's assistance and used Peter's boat for a better vantage point in addressing the crowds. After speaking, he told Peter to move out to deep water and let down his nets. In others words, do something you haven't done before. Take new risks. Go to new places. Try new things.

My friend Bill McGraw has a place on Lake Erie. One day he said, "Mike, you have to take a couple of days and go walleye fishing with me."

So, I took him up on his offer. We got up long before daylight, loaded the boat, and set out. I couldn't believe how easy it was. I had my first keeper on the second cast. We caught our limit by nine and didn't even need the lunch we had packed. The "Erie Dearie" lures worked just the way the guy at the bait shop told us they would.

I could hardly wait to get back to Bill's place the next spring for walleye season. We didn't even pack a lunch. After all, we were in hours before lunch the year before. Well, our prior experience of success did not serve us very well on this occasion. We repeated the same routine, hit the same spots, and used the same lures, but we had only three bites and caught only one small perch by noon. We finished the long day with only one walleye between us to show for all our hard work. We docked the boat and discovered from the day's more successful fisher folks that the fish were biting about two miles farther out from where we had been trolling. Lesson learned: you can't keep fishing in the same places.

Consider the result when Peter was willing to cast out into new places: They caught so many fish that their nets began to break, and they had to call for help! There is an important analogy here. If you want to be an effective disciple of Jesus Christ or "fisher of people," you have to be willing to move out of your comfort zone, try new things, and enlist the help of others.

How is God calling you to move out of your comfort zone in order to spread the word?

CONTAGIOUS CHRISTIANITY

"In the same way, let your light shine before others, so that they may see your good works and give glory to your Father in heaven." (Matthew 5:16 NRSV)

Recently, my colleague Jeff and I were eating lunch at Skyline Chili. Naturally, you try to be careful while eating but it's so easy to get sauce splashed on your shirt. So Jeff and I were eating and Jeff got a big, messy glob on his shirt. We didn't have any time to change clothes before our meeting, so he pulls this little thing out—it's like a marker, but filled with bleach, and like magic, the spot disappeared right before my very eyes! I said, "I need one of those!" That's called viral marketing—one friend shows another, and seeing is believing. It's a lot more effective than a canned speech about the product's features and benefits.

Spreading the gospel is the same way. When the people around us see Jesus alive and at work in our lives, they want to experience him too. That's viral evangelism—seeing is believing.

Jesus told his followers to "go and make disciples," first at home and then to the ends of the earth. Acts 2:44-47 describes how those followers lived after Jesus left them with that command, and we see how their lifestyle attracted new disciples. They shared things in common and lived peacefully with one another. What a powerful witness, in a world filled with greed and discord!

If you are seeking to follow Jesus in the path of discipleship, your call is to love God, to love others, and to serve the world. This is also the way that you make disciples. If you are following Jesus as a faithful disciple, your life and the love you demonstrate will be contagious, a living example of Christ's love to those around you. Disciples produce disciples. The important thing is not how many people you lead to become followers of Jesus; if you focus on actively and effectively serving Christ's mission by being his hands and feet in your community and the world, then you *will* make disciples!

Is your life a faithful example of Jesus' love for the world?
How can you live a more "contagious" faith?

A NEW KIND OF MISSIONARY

> *"But you will receive power when the Holy Spirit comes
> on you; and you will be my witnesses in Jerusalem, and
> in all Judea and Samaria, and to the ends of the earth."*
> (Acts 1:8)

The Fort McKinley neighborhood lies within the western boundaries of the Dayton city limits. The neighborhood is comprised of small homes built in the 1930s and 1940s for young working-class families who labored in a city driven by automobile factories. Many had migrated north from the Appalachian ranges of West Virginia, Kentucky, and Tennessee to share in a piece of the American dream. As families grew and the auto industry thrived, these families began to migrate out with the suburban sprawl. The transition during the civil unrest of the 1960s and 1970s hastened the working-class exodus. The neighborhood transitioned from working-class families who owned their homes to a low income, racially diverse neighborhood of tenants. In the 1980s and 1990s, families who left the Fort McKinley neighborhood for the suburbs were still driving back to their old neighborhood church, but by 2007 attendance had dropped drastically.

Ginghamsburg Church is sixteen miles from the low-income neighborhood of Fort McKinley. Eighty of our members saw this as an opportunity to become a new kind of missionary and agreed to make Fort McKinley United Methodist Church their place of worship and service. In just three months, the new congregation had to begin a second worship celebration!

By leaving their comfort zone and pouring their energy into the Fort McKinley community, those eighty "urban missionaries" have been able to meet an enormous number of real, felt needs among struggling people. They are meeting immediate physical needs through food pantries, a grocery co-op, a senior lunch program, and free community meals four days a week. Gently used clothing and furniture stores and car and medical supply ministries seek to provide urgent care. Some funds are also available to help clients with utility bills. The goal of this kind of work is to connect people to the liberating love of Jesus and to empower folks to rise out of the malaise of poverty.

Are you willing to become a new kind of missionary—a missionary who becomes invested in meeting needs and changing lives close to home? Jesus told his disciples to be his witnesses first in Jerusalem, then in nearby Judea and Samaria, and finally throughout the world. Will you answer the call? By joining together with others, you can revitalize a community in need and change the world.

Could you be a missionary close to home? What can you do to begin revitalizing a community near you? Who will you enlist to help you?

SEEING AND DOING

*How does God's love abide in anyone who has
the world's goods and sees a brother or sister in
need and yet refuses help?
Little children, let us love, not in word or speech, but in
truth and action. (1 John 3:17-18 NRSV)*

Spreading the word is faith in action—it is seeing a need and then doing something about it. My friend Neil Cole says, "If you want to win this world to Christ, you are going to have to sit in the smoking section." Following Christ and carrying on his mission in the world is an ongoing process of "see" and "do." We must move out of the waiting rooms of our own little worlds into the emergency rooms of the real world to serve human needs and share the gospel of Jesus Christ.

John, one of Jesus' first followers, said that God's love cannot abide in us if we see the needs of others but do not respond, offering practical help. We are to spread the word of Christ and the love of Christ not only in word or speech but also in truth and action.

Too often our efforts at evangelism focus on urging people to make a confession of faith—to declare that Jesus is Lord. But Jesus warned, "Not everyone who says to me, 'Lord, Lord,' will enter the kingdom of heaven, but only the one who does the will of my Father in heaven" (Matthew 7:21 NRSV). A declaration of faith is good, but more important is the way that faith transforms the way we see the world and our response to the need we see.

Statistics from 2009 revealed that 43.6 million Americans were living in poverty (14.3 percent): 15.5 million children under the age of eighteen (20.7 percent) were in poverty; 3.4 million seniors aged sixty-five and older (8.9 percent) were in poverty; and in 2008, 4.8 million U.S. households (4.1 percent) accessed emergency food from a food pantry one or more times.[5]

The world is watching to see how we will respond. Will our faith in the One who loves the world enough to sacrifice himself lead us to live sacrificially as well? Will we see and overlook—perhaps saying a prayer and thinking we have done all we can—or will we see and do?

What is one need you have seen but have not yet done anything to help address? What can you do to help make a real difference?

NO STRINGS ATTACHED

*"If you lend to those from whom you hope to receive, what
credit is that to you? Even sinners lend to sinners, to receive
as much again. But love your enemies, do good, and lend,
expecting nothing in return." (Luke 6:34-35a NRSV)*

Jermaine is a thirty-two-year-old fisherman in Port Maria,
Jamaica, who has made his living from a simple wood
boat since his early teens. Homeless and living on the beach
before age thirteen, Jermaine was befriended by local fishermen and taught how to fish. At eighteen he started col-
lecting debris and pieces of wood from the sea to build the
simple shack where he and his family currently reside.

Jermaine received a microbusiness loan through a group
of small-business owners working in cooperation with a
partnership between Ginghamsburg Church and an organi-
zation in Atlanta (ACE). A loan of $400 was given to
Jermaine after the business owners helped him to develop a
business plan. He used the money to work on his boat and

overhaul the motor. Part of the business plan included using his boat to take tourists out to a reef for snorkeling. Jermaine paid back the loan with 5 percent interest.

When I met Jermaine, he was presenting a second business plan for a loan of $500, which would allow him to purchase ten fish traps that would be working for him while he was running the tourist side of the business. This would increase his production and revenue by growing his customer base with the local hotels. The next phase would allow him to employ a few friends and family members, touching the lives of twenty people.

Before leaving we learned that Jermaine's baby was sick. We took the child with Jermaine and his wife to the local church where our team was running a clinic. Jermaine was reluctant to come inside. I could tell "church" was foreign to him, and he was wary of our motives. He entered, and was given a warm welcome. The baby was treated, and Jermaine and his wife received dental treatment. We introduced them to the local pastor and reminded them that we were not only their business partners but would be serving them through the local church to help meet all the needs in their lives.

Many people today are skeptical of Christians. They have heard what we're against but not what we're for. They have seen us provide help with strings attached. It's easy to be frustrated with misconceptions people have about our faith, but Jesus said people would be able to sort out truth from fiction by the demonstration of his followers' love. Show love with no strings attached, and people will see Jesus shining through.

> *Do you worry about how Christianity is perceived?*
> *How can your actions set the record straight without*
> *saying a word?*

SERVING COURAGEOUSLY

COURAGE IN THE AGE OF ANXIETY

Be on guard. Stand firm in the faith. Be courageous.
Be strong. (1 Corinthians 16:13 NLT)

Historians will identify the years following the terrorist attacks of September 11, 2001, as an "age of anxiety." Anxiety is an irrational by-product of fear, based on current circumstances or perceived future events. Reactive responses that result from these unchecked emotions can cause us to act outside of our moral ideals. America's invasion of Iraq, based on the perception of weapons of mass destruction, or torture as a means of extracting information from suspected terrorists are two examples of American actions that could not have occurred apart from the levels of anxiety created by the terrorist attacks of 9/11.

Just take a look at the economic factors that have fueled emotional levels of anxiety. There was the near collapse of the worldwide banking system that resulted from the 2008 failures of some of the largest global banks and investment companies. Then there was unemployment created by the bankruptcies, buyouts, and closings of Fortune 500 companies and the resulting future tax burden created by the largest government bailout in history. The number of U.S. home foreclosures grew by 24 percent during the first three months of 2009 and would continue to rise further.[6] Economists are using the scary "D" word as a future possibility. We are waking up to the reality that the Great Depression that our grandparents experienced might have only been the prelude to an apocalyptic global tomorrow.

The instability of the global political climate only serves to intensify our human tendency to seek refuge in the security of our own emotional and ideological fortresses. The boarding process at any airport accompanied by the graded levels of alert is a constant reminder of imminent attack. Nuclear proliferation in North Korea and Iran, the growth of militant Islam and its spread in the Western world can lead us as followers of Jesus to place our trust in the militant means of "chariots and horses" instead of the Lord our God. We also must be on guard against the tendency to allow fearful emotions due to the current global economic climate to insulate us from the plights and injustices experienced by the poor.

At the heart of every decision we make as Christians is a choice between anxiety and courage. Our fears and anxieties tell us to take care of ourselves, hoard resources, and avoid putting ourselves in risky situations. Courage reminds us that God is always with us, calling us to the dangerous places to do his will in a hurting world.

What are you most afraid of? How does God's voice counter the voice of fear?

YOUR LEGACY

"Before I made you in your mother's womb, I chose you.
Before you were born, I set you apart for a special work."
(Jeremiah 1:5 NCV)

L ife is brief and fleeting. Recently I celebrated my thirty-
first anniversary since coming to Ginghamsburg
Church. It seems like it was just two or three years ago. In
my trips around the country I run into some of my friends
and acquaintances whom I haven't seen since my seminary
days. Isn't it amazing how people change in physical appear-
ance from their middle twenties to late fifties? Especially
when we haven't seen each other in thirty plus years. Life is
short!

There is a cemetery behind my house where I regularly
take contemplative walks with my dog. I look at the tomb-
stones and wonder about the lives and stories of the people
whose lifetimes are simply marked by the year of birth and
death. My walks through the cemetery are reminders of

both the gift and brevity of life, and the realization that life is really defined by the dash between the two dates.

Your life is a gift from God. It is what each of us does in the dash that becomes our gift back. You may feel like you have nothing to give, or that your gift isn't worthy. God does not agree. You were made by an awesome Creator who designed you to do something great. Don't conform to the timid ways of the world. We have a choice between courage and conformity. Will we boldly take the difficult road and challenge ourselves to go beyond our comfort zones into the places of Christ's calling? Or, will we settle for the status quo, bowing to the pressures and practices of our culture? The choice is ours. God says, "I have set before you life and death, blessings and curses. Now choose life, so that you and your children may live" (Deuteronomy 30:19).

Live boldly, and your legacy will live well beyond your physical lifetime. We are all here to serve a purpose in God's redemptive mission. Don't waste the gift. There are no comebacks or do-overs. Your time is now!

What do you see as your unique role in life and in God's redemptive mission in the world? What do you need to do in order to serve this purpose with boldness and joy?

STEP OUT OF THE BOAT

*Early in the morning he came walking toward them on the
sea. But when the disciples saw him walking on the sea,
they were terrified, saying, "It is a ghost!" And they cried
out in fear. But immediately Jesus spoke to them and said,
"Take heart, it is I; do not be afraid."*
(Matthew 14:25-27 NRSV)

L ife is scary, with challenges so daunting that we may just
want to stay in bed and pull the covers over our heads.
Jesus' call to join him out in the stormy sea doesn't sound
like a walk in the park, but if we refuse, we'll miss out on
some of God's greatest blessings for our lives.

To experience life you must take risks. One of my favorite
biblical stories is when Peter stepped out of the boat and
attempted to walk on water. There wasn't anything about
the act that made sense. His fellow disciples saw it as rash
and impulsive. When he began to sink, I'm sure there were
plenty of, "I told you so's" and "I knew the fool was crazy."
Why did Peter do it? Peter stepped out of the boat because

he heard Jesus say, "Come!" Like the eleven disciples who stayed in the boat, most will miss the wonder of a miraculous life mission because they will never act beyond the confines of the lifeboat or outside of the expectations of those traveling with them.

If you allow fear to determine your decisions and actions, you will lose your life. Why do people stay in destructive, abusive relationships? Why do people stay in jobs they hate instead of taking the risks to pursue a lifelong passion? Why don't people stand up and speak out and act in the face of injustice? It all comes down to one word: fear.

That is why the first words out of Jesus' mouth after the resurrection were, "Don't be afraid!" There is no circumstance, world leader, or group that can derail the righteous purpose of God. The purpose of God for a time might be delayed, but it will not be denied. God will have the last word! Faith is persistently hoping in God's promised outcome and committing to the necessary actions to achieve it.

In what areas are you allowing fear to determine your decisions and actions? What actions do you need to take in order to "step out of the boat"?

MORE THAN FEELINGS

He replied, "You of little faith, why are you so afraid?"
Then he got up and rebuked the winds and the waves, and it
was completely calm. (Matthew 8:26)

Faith is not the absence of fear. Faith is feeling the fear and then acting on the promises and purpose of God anyway. Faith is when every cell in your body is screaming "Run!" while you continue to follow forward in obedience, praying, "Not my will, Lord, but your will be done." Faith is the proactive response—in spite of those feelings and uncertainties—to the mandates of heaven.

Mother Teresa is one of the best testaments to the reality of Jesus' presence in the world that I have witnessed in my lifetime, but few knew that she had experienced a sense of "the absence of the presence of God" for almost the entirety of her ministry (read *Come Be My Light* for more about her experience).

Her first years as a nun were spent teaching in parochial schools. She spoke of having an experience in 1946 when Christ spoke to her and said, "Come be my light to the poorest of poor." She spent the next two years prayerfully seeking the counsel of her superiors and formulating a mission strategy. In 1950 she founded the Missionaries of Charity and began to minister to the poorest of the poor in the streets of Calcutta. But from 1948 until her death in 1997, she felt that Jesus' presence had abandoned her. In her letters to her confessors she referred to Jesus as "the Great Absent One" and said it seemed that his relationship to her was like that of "the comatose spouse." In 1953 she wrote to her confessor: "Please pray for me that I may not spoil his work and that our Lord may show himself—for there is such terrible darkness within me, as if everything was dead. It has been like this more or less from the time I started the work."[7] For forty-nine years, except for a brief five-week period she mentions in 1959, one of the greatest missionaries of all time felt the absence of God's presence.

Can you imagine the hole that would be left in the fabric of the world if Mother Teresa had acted on her feelings rather than the mandate of the gospel? The absence of feeling does not mean the absence of God. Feelings are not required for faith and may be misleading. Faith is not the absence of doubt or fear. Faith is acting on God's word in spite of doubt and fear.

What do you feel with regard to God right now? If you are feeling somehow negative, what step of faith do you need to take in spite of your feelings?

FACING NAYSAYERS

"Be strong and courageous. Do not be terrified; do not be discouraged, for the LORD *your God will be with you wherever you go." (Joshua 1:9)*

God called his people to act courageously in times of chaos. The children of God had allowed the paralysis of fear to turn what should have been an exodus trip of a few months into a forty-year waste of a lifetime for a whole generation. When they reached the land of God's promise, Joshua and Caleb were the only two who were willing to trust God despite the discouraging report of the majority. As Joshua was preparing to lead the new generation into the land of God's promise, here is what God said to Joshua:

> "Be strong and courageous; for you shall put this people in possession of the land that I swore to their ancestors to give them. Only be strong and very courageous, being careful to act in accordance with all the law that my servant Moses commanded you; do not turn from it

to the right hand or to the left, so that you may be successful wherever you go." (Joshua 1:6-7 NRSV)

There is an important lesson here for all of us. Don't follow the lead of naysayers or negative resisters or you will be buried in the wilderness with them! There will always be people who disagree with you, people who say you are crazy or unreasonable. If you dream big, there will be people who want to downsize your dream, who say it is impossible. Seek the wisdom of godly mentors, who will seek God's vision with you, and not seek to tear you down in the process.

It is easy to let the mean-spiritedness and faithlessness of naysayers around us negate the mandates and purposes of God. We must courageously face them, standing firm on the promise that God is with us wherever we go.

Who are the naysayers or negative resisters in your life right now? What are they discouraging you from doing or pursuing—whether intentionally or unintentionally? What would it mean for you to courageously face them?

EXCUSES AND EXPECTATIONS

The angel said to the women, "Do not be afraid; I know that you are looking for Jesus who was crucified. He is not here; for he has been raised, as he said. Come, see the place where he lay." (Matthew 28:5-6 NRSV)

The women came to the tomb expecting to find a corpse and instead witnessed a world-changing miracle. Jesus was not there. He had risen!

The place where Jesus had been laid was a cemetery. What do you expect to find in a cemetery? Death. God's best work is done in places of death. This is why as God's people we need to be camped right in the middle of the Darfurs of this world, serving courageously in places of pain and need.

I have discovered that the fruits of a person's life and work rise to the level of his or her expectations. "As a person thinks within himself or herself, so he or she is" (Proverbs 23:7, paraphrased). Many Christians think that they can't begin to have anywhere near the impact that someone else might have because of their lack of education or position or power or money or support. No doubt you have heard many "I can't because—" excuses from others in your lifetime, and you've probably said it a few times yourself!

As a church pastor, I've faced all kinds of obstacles over the years. Ginghamsburg Church is located in a community of twenty-two houses, sixteen miles north of one of the ten fastest dying cities in the U.S. The population has declined during my thirty-plus-year tenure. There were fewer than one hundred people in the church when I arrived and only thirty left after that first year. I inherited a $27,000 budget, was met with resistance, and still have days when I feel like throwing in the towel. It is during those times that I remind myself that God does God's best work in desperate situations. God is the God of abundance, love, life, and provision. Not even death can deny God's redemptive plan. There is no circumstance that can change the promise or purposes of God!

You don't need different circumstances or new surroundings. You don't need a better education, more training, or a different job. You don't need a different spouse. You don't need a bigger or better house or more money. It's time to get rid of your excuses and lay claim to some world-changing expectations!

What excuses are keeping you from serving courageously and making a difference for God's kingdom work? What higher expectations can you set for yourself?

HOLY GROUND

*Then Jacob woke from his sleep and said, "Surely the LORD
is in this place—and I did not know it!" And he was afraid,
and said, "How awesome is this place! This is none other
than the house of God, and this is the gate of heaven."*
(Genesis 28:16-17 NRSV)

Jacob had a dream in which God promised to bless the
land on which he was lying (Genesis 28:13). God told
him that all the people of the earth would be blessed
through him and his descendants. When he woke up he
knew the Lord was there with him, and he called the place
the gate of heaven. Like Jacob, it's time for us to wake up
and recognize that God is in this place. We are standing at
the gate of heaven to be the conduit of heaven's resources
for the least and the lost throughout the world.

Jacob was traveling through a barren land when God
spoke to him in this way. He was using a rock as a pillow
when God appeared in his dream! It can be difficult to see

the holiness in life's harsh places. Places of loneliness, depression, poverty, and disease seem at first glance to hold nothing but evil and despair. But look closer, and God is already there. Wherever you are right now, you are in God's place in God's time. The place where you are standing is holy ground! The whole earth is full of God's glory and God's potential to heal and restore hope.

Like Jacob and his descendents, the whole world can be blessed through us. Jesus has taught us and empowered us to be his hands and feet. There is a world out there in need, but God has a plan for meeting those needs and restoring the dark places—us! This simple yet profound realization will empower you to serve courageously for the sake of the gospel message and mission of Jesus Christ.

Have you ever felt that you were standing on holy ground?
How will the world be blessed through your faithful response
to Christ's call?

NOTES

1. From his work *The Church as the People of God*. I took it from Alan Hirsch's *The Forgotten Ways* (Grand Rapids: Brazos Press, 2006), 15.

2. David Kinnaman and Gabe Lyons, *Unchristian: What a New Generation Really Thinks About Christianity* (Grand Rapids: Baker Books, 2007), 15.

3. Alan Hirsch, *The Forgotten Ways* (Grand Rapids: Brazos Press, 2006), 122.

4. Wikipedia, "Imprinting." http://en.wikipedia.org/wiki/Imprinting_(psychology)

5. See Feeding America, http://feedingamerica.org//faces-of-hunger/hunger-101/hunger-and-poverty-statistics.aspx.

6. Associated Press, "US Home Foreclosures Jump 24% in First Quarter; Housing Starts Fall 10.8%" *NY Daily News*, April 16 2009.

7. See Mother Teresa, *Come Be My Light: The Private Writings of the "Saint of Calcutta,"* ed. Brian Kolodiejchuk (New York: Doubleday, 2007).